'Til His
KINGDOM
Comes
Living in the Last Days

CHARLES R. SWINDOLL
JOHN F. WALVOORD

INSIGHT FOR LIVING

'Til His Kingdom Comes: Living in the Last Days

By Charles R. Swindoll and John F. Walvoord

An Issues and Answers Collection

From the Bible-Teaching Ministry of Charles R. Swindoll

Published by IFL Publishing House, A Division of Insight for Living
Post Office Box 251007, Plano, Texas 75025-1007

Chapter one was adapted from Charles R. Swindoll, "The Future of God's Plan," in *Insight's Bible Companion: Practical Helps for Better Study*, vol. 2 (Anaheim, Calif.: Insight for Living, 2000), 1–5.

Chapter two was adapted from a pamphlet by Dr. John F. Walvoord, *The Last Days: Impending World Events in Prophecy* (Dallas: Dallas Theological Seminary, 1998).

Chapter three was adapted from Charles R. Swindoll, "Practical Advice for Perilous Times," in *The Road to Armageddon* (Nashville: Word Publishing, a unit of Thomas Nelson, Inc., 1999), 1–21.

Editor in Chief: Cynthia Swindoll, President, Insight for Living
Executive Vice President: Wayne Stiles, Th.M., D.Min., Dallas Theological Seminary
Director of Creative Ministries: Michael J. Svigel, Th.M., Ph.D. candidate, Dallas Theological Seminary
Editor: Brie Engeler, B.A., University Scholars, Baylor University
Copy Editors: Jim Craft, M.A., English, Mississippi College
 Melanie Munnell, M.A., Humanities, The University of Texas at Dallas
Proofreader: Joni Halpin, B.S., Accountancy, Miami University
Project Coordinator, Creative Ministries: Cari Harris, B.A., Journalism, Grand Canyon University
Project Coordinator, Communications: Dusty R. Crosby, B.S., Communication, Dallas Baptist University
Cover Designer: Steven Tomlin, Embry-Riddle Aeronautical University, 1992–1995
Production Artist: Nancy Gustine, B.F.A., Advertising Art, University of North Texas

Cover Image: Copyright © 2007 by JupiterImages Corporation.

ISBN: 978-1-57972-768-0

Printed in the United States of America

Table of Contents

About the Authors

Charles R. Swindoll

Charles R. Swindoll has devoted his life to the clear, practical teaching and application of God's Word and His grace. A pastor at heart, Chuck has served as senior pastor to congregations in Texas, Massachusetts, and California. He currently pastors Stonebriar Community Church in Frisco, Texas, but Chuck's listening audience extends far beyond a local church body. As a leading program in Christian broadcasting, *Insight for Living* airs in major Christian radio markets around the world, reaching people groups in languages they can understand. Chuck's extensive writing ministry has also served the body of Christ worldwide, and his leadership as president and now chancellor of Dallas Theological Seminary has helped prepare and equip a new generation for ministry. Chuck and Cynthia, his partner in life and ministry, have four grown children and ten grandchildren.

John F. Walvoord

Dr. John F. Walvoord (1910–2002), a leading spokesman for biblical prophecy, was a graduate of Wheaton College (B.A., 1931; D.D., 1960), Texas Christian University (M.A., 1945), and Dallas Theological Seminary (Th.B., Th.M., 1934; Th.D., 1936). Recognized throughout the world as an outstanding educator, author, and Bible conference speaker, he served as the second president of Dallas Theological Seminary from 1952–1986, and as chancellor and later, chancellor emeritus, from 1986 until entering into the presence of his Lord in 2002.

The Alpha and Omega

ΑΩ

Notice the Alpha and Omega symbol on the cover of this book. These are the first and last letters of the Greek alphabet, and when used together, they signify completeness. God describes Himself with this symbol in Revelation 1:8.

> "I am the Alpha and the Omega," says the Lord God, "who is and who was and who is to come, the Almighty."

The "Alpha and Omega" remind us that the God of the Bible is the one true God. He knows the end from the beginning, and His sovereign plan for the ages can never fail (Isaiah 41:4; 44:6–8). Christ announced His coming with these powerful words:

> "Behold, I am coming quickly, and My reward is with Me, to render to every man according to what he has done. I am the Alpha and the Omega, the first and the last, the beginning and the end." (Revelation 22:12–13)

Introduction: Living in the Last Days

Take a moment and let the images of the last several years run through your mind. Violence in Israel . . . September 11 . . . wars in the Middle East . . . the Indonesian Tsunami . . . incurable viruses . . . Hurricane Katrina . . . global terrorism . . .

As these and other snapshots of current events flash through our minds, we can't help but wonder, "Are we living in the last days?"

The answer is *yes*.

Now, before you run into the wilderness to hide or climb a mountain to be the first to meet the Lord in the air, let us explain. Since the day of Pentecost (AD 33), the church has been in the "last days" (Acts 2:17; Hebrews 1:2; 1 John 2:18). When the Holy Spirit came to empower the disciples to be witnesses for Christ, God's end-time clock began to count down. From that day forward, the final alarm could have sounded literally at any moment. Simply put, *nothing needs to happen before God's trumpet sounds and the end-time prophecies begin to unfold.* No war, disease, technological breakthrough, political development, religious deception, or other event *must* happen to allow the final judgments to begin.

Yet this fact hasn't stopped end-time enthusiasts from pointing to current events and saying, "This is it! That's the final empire! That's the Antichrist! That's a clear sign that the end is near!" Though the events we see in the news *could* lead to the final crossroads of human history, until the judgments actually begin, nobody can know this for sure.

This unique resource, *'Til His Kingdom Comes: Living in the Last Days*, is designed to answer some of the most pressing questions about prophecy that keep us scratching our heads. But it does more than just outline future events. It is also intended to calm unreasonable fears about the future, instilling hope and confidence in the God who not only knows the end from the beginning but also wants to be intimately involved in your life *today*.

Much more could be said about the relevance of God's prophetic plans in your present life, but we've narrowed it down to what every believer should know about the end times . . . *and why*.

'Til His
KINGDOM
Comes
Living in the Last Days

The Future of God's Plan: A Panorama
by Charles R. Swindoll

Let's admit it—the future can be worrisome. It isn't the past that gives us our greatest anxiety. It isn't even the present that disturbs us the most. It's the unseen tomorrow. It's that area in which we really have questions about who is in control. Hindsight invariably has twenty-twenty vision. Looking back, things make sense. But looking into tomorrow, we can't see anything.

More often than not, people usually look to God's Word for what *has* happened, not necessarily for what is *going to* happen. But I have great news for you, my friend! Scripture can be trusted at both ends of God's program. In God's chronological program, all will end well. We want to know—especially when life is hard or when we agonize over history's unfair twists and turns—that everything is going to turn out okay. We want the assurance that prophecy provides. The God whom we serve and in whom we believe is not on the edge of heaven wondering, "What in the world is taking place down there?" or "How did that nation get into that condition?" or "What am I going to do about it?"

If nothing else, let our discussion of the earth's last days affirm to you that our heavenly Father knows precisely what is going to happen. His timepiece runs in precise, perfect order.

Prophecy: A Balanced Approach

Those who study prophecy can easily become tempted toward great imbalance, which is usually revealed in two areas. The first is a desire to predict exact dates (common among prophecy fanatics). They say, "The Lord will return in the year _____," and they fill in the blank. The other extreme that goes along with it is a smug, super-spiritual, I-know-it-all-as-it-relates-to-the-future attitude. You're not going to find either of these extremes in this or any other prophetic study from Insight for Living.

When I'm gone, if I'm long since forgotten for most everything else, I hope I will be remembered for one thing: balance. My one great desire before God is to be a balanced man, a balanced preacher, and a balanced expositor—not always in the Old Testament, and not always in the New Testament. Not always on the subject of prophecy, and not always ignoring prophecy. Not always on some profound part of the spiritual life, and yet not always overlooking it, either. I want to apply that same balance to our study of God's future events. As one of my mentors used to say, "We've been given this prophetic Word not just to satisfy idle curiosity, but also to change lives."

A Great Time to Live

In the panorama of this world's timeline, we live in the church age. God gave birth to the church in Acts 2. And we have the joy and the privilege of living in a time in which the Spirit of God universally indwells all of His children, His Word is open and understood, and evangelism is sweeping through many parts of the world. It's a marvelous era in which to live — so different from the days of the Law with sacrifices and a rigid lifestyle. The freedom of grace, the beauty of worship, and so many technical capabilities that we just take for granted—we experience all of these in the church age.

This time stands out from other times in history for three distinct reasons: first of all, there is no longer a distinction between Jew or Gentile in the church. The same is true whether you come to know Christ as a religious Jew or as a pagan Gentile. You still come into the family of God. This was never true back in the days of the Law.

Second, we do not know how long the age in which we now live will last. Scripture reveals no exit date, regardless of what anyone may tell you.

Third, this era will end with Christ's return for His bride, the church. This event is often called the rapture.

The Next Event: The Rapture

I'm absolutely convinced we are in the very last days of the church. This church age in which we find ourselves will end with the rapture of the church.

For your own perusal in days to come, let me give you some Scriptures that describe the last days of the church. Read each one slowly, carefully: 1 Corinthians 15:50–58; John 14:1–3; and 1 Thessalonians 4:13–18. Just to throw you students of prophecy a curve, add Revelation 3:10, which so clearly describes why I'm interpreting the timing of the rapture the way that I am according to Scripture. Here, the church is promised they will be taken out from (literally, "out from among") the time of great testing that will sweep the whole world. It's a unique promise that teaches the rapture and its place in God's prophetic plan.

Now, let me give you a couple of distinctions regarding the rapture. First, all living and dead believers (the key word is *believers*) will be removed from planet earth. The second distinction is rather obvious: only unbelievers will be left on the earth. Believers who are living at the time of the rapture will be literally caught up to be with Christ when He returns for us.

As I see it, the rapture is the next major event in God's future program. I anticipate it every day. The anticipation comes to me more often when I'm under great testing than when things are going well. It's a great hope, a great comfort, and a great encouragement. Listen to the words of Paul:

> But we do not want you to be uninformed, brethren, about those who are asleep, so that you will not grieve as do the rest who have no hope. For if we believe that Jesus died and rose again, even so God will bring with Him those who have fallen asleep in Jesus. For this we say to you by the word of the Lord, that we who are alive and remain until the coming of the Lord, will not precede those who have fallen asleep. (1 Thessalonians 4:13–15)

He then gives the order of events:

> For the Lord Himself will descend from heaven with a shout, with the voice of the archangel and with the trumpet of God, and the dead in Christ will rise first. Then we who are alive and remain will be caught up together with them in the clouds

to meet the Lord in the air, and so we shall always be with the Lord. (1 Thessalonians 4:16–17)

Brothers and sisters in the church age, that's hope! Living and dead will be changed *instantly* and *permanently* as we're taken to be with the Lord *eternally*. Do you know what else it spells? It spells disaster. Now, why? Because it leaves this old earth in chaotic conditions. With all believers taken away, can you imagine the turmoil, the confusion in homes and businesses, and the half-full churches?

Some of you reading this, quite frankly, will be left, because up to this point in your life, you've never come to know Jesus Christ. You may be counting on church membership, or a good moral background, or being around Christians to get you into heaven. You've not yet humbled your heart before God and expressed a prayer like this: "I'm a sinner. I need hope. I need help. I need forgiveness. I need Your love. I need Your grace. Today—right at this moment—I take Jesus as my Savior . . . my Master . . . my own Redeemer." (To learn more about accepting Christ as your Savior, see "How to Begin a Relationship with God" beginning on page 71.)

I plead with you, if you learn nothing else from prophecy, learn the importance of being ready for His coming. The only way to be ready is to be in Christ. Ready or not, He's coming! He is coming soon! And His coming could be *any time*, day or night. Every evidence on the surface of Scripture, as well as in our times, implies that His presence draws near. He could even come today before the clock strikes midnight. Wouldn't that be great?

Child of God, your future is in God's hands. All the world's future events are in His hands. His sovereign arrangement of those future events replaces fear with peace. He has a handle on the order in which they will transpire. And the Bible teaches that our times are in His hands. One of the greatest verses I've ever learned is:

> "All the inhabitants of the earth are accounted as nothing,
> But He does according to His will in the host of heaven
> And among the inhabitants of earth;
> And no one can ward off His hand
> Or say to Him, 'What have you done?'" (Daniel 4:35)

Isn't that a magnificent statement! When we wonder, "God, what are You doing?" Daniel says, "Even when you can't understand it, His plan is unfolding. Count on it. He knows what He's about."

Because God knows what He's about, you and I can trust Him with tomorrow. So? *So trust Him!*

TIMELINE OF FUTURE EVENTS

Rapture of Believers
I Thess. 4:13–18

Judgment Seat of Christ
2 Cor. 5:10

Second Coming of Christ
Rev. 19:11–21
Matt. 25:31–46

Great White Throne Judgment
Rev. 20:11–15

Divine Judgments
Seals…Trumpets…Bowls

Israel's Restoration

NEW HEAVEN AND NEW EARTH
Rev. 21–22

Abomination of Desolation

Armageddon
Rev. 16:13–16

Gospel Preached to the Nations	3 1/2 Years of Deception	3 1/2 Years of the Antichrist's Reign	Christ Reigns on the Earth	
CHURCH AGE From Day of Pentecost to the Rapture	**SEVEN-YEAR TRIBULATION** Dan. 9:27; 11:36–39; 2 Thess. 2:1–8 Matt. 24:15; Rev. 4–19		**MILLENNIAL KINGDOM** 1,000 Years of Peace on Earth Rev. 20:1–8	**ETERNITY**

Impending World Events in Prophecy
by John F. Walvoord

The fact that one-fourth of the Bible was predictive when it was written emphasizes the importance of prophecy to the Christian faith. This attitude of expectation not only keeps Christians alert to impending events but also reassures them of the ultimate victory of their faith. After all, the very nature of the Christian faith provides hope for this life as well as the life to come.

Central to all prophecy is the second coming of Christ. It is the most frequently mentioned event of the New Testament and has been incorporated in all the orthodox creeds, whether Roman Catholic, Greek Orthodox, or Protestant. In fact, each contains the statement that Jesus Christ is literally coming again to judge the world.

The four essential prophetic programs that accompany the Second Coming are the rapture and God's plans for Israel, the nations, and the church. Their dramatic unfolding serves as the backdrop for impending world events.

Problems in Prophetic Interpretation

Confusion has arisen over these great end-time events because of the failure of interpreters to follow three basic rules of biblical interpretation. First, the Bible is completely inspired of God and is without error. Second, a literal interpretation is the only method by which a prophetic program can be understood. Unfortunately, in the history of the church many interpreters have held that prophecy is not literal, which has led to chaos in much of the prophetic interpretation of the Bible. Third, the details of prophecy need to be carefully observed.

The danger in disregarding these rules is seen in the misunderstanding of the Old Testament teaching that the first and second comings of Christ were two separate events. This mistake was reached by overlooking the details of the first coming. It was not until Christ actually died that the disciples understood that there was a first coming in which He would suffer and die and a second coming in which He would gloriously reign.

Conversely, following these rules supports bedrock beliefs such as Christ's second coming to rule over the earth for a thousand years and that the rapture of the church will occur before the Great Tribulation. Moreover, the fact that those biblical prophecies already fulfilled were fulfilled literally indicates this is God's method of fulfilling predicted events. That the rapture of the church is imminent is a fundamental practical fact of the Christian faith.

The Rapture of the Church

The rapture of the church was not revealed in the Old Testament. In fact, no events are ever recorded in Scripture as signs or anticipations of the rapture. Rather, it was first revealed when Christ told His disciples, "And if

I go and prepare a place for you, I will come back and take you to be with me that you also may be where I am" (John 14:3 NIV). This was the first announcement of the coming of Christ to take His saints out of the world and was totally contrary to what the disciples believed. They were expecting Christ to bring in immediately a kingdom on earth.

Later Paul added additional details:

> For the Lord himself will come down from heaven, with a loud command, with the voice of the archangel and with the trumpet call of God, and the dead in Christ will rise first. After that, we who are still alive and are left will be caught up together with them in the clouds to meet the Lord in the air. And so we will be with the Lord forever. (1 Thessalonians 4:16–17 NIV)

So according to this Scripture, Christ returns bodily from heaven to the air above the earth and causes the dead in Christ to rise as well as the living to be changed. The term *rapture* is just another English word for being "caught up together with them" and the translation could be that we are "raptured together with them in the clouds to meet the Lord in the air."

Through the centuries the church has anticipated the possibility of Christ coming any day and fulfilling the doctrine of the rapture. While the world will not see the glory of Christ until the Second Coming, Christians will see the glory of Christ immediately (1 John 3:2) and at the same time be transformed into His likeness (1 Corinthians 15:51–53) when they are caught up in the rapture.

The Last Trumpet and the Seventh Trumpet

Some scholars equate the "last trumpet" announcing the rapture of the church in 1 Corinthians 15:52 with the seventh trumpet of Revelation 11:15. However, a close examination reveals that these two trumpets refer to separate events.

The seventh trumpet of Revelation 11:15 announces the final phase of the wrath of God, the beginning of Christ's reign, and the praises of the heavenly chorus in response to this exchange of power. In contrast, Paul's trumpet of 1 Corinthians 15:52 refers to the bodily resurrection and the "catching up" of believing saints.

We must also remember that Paul wrote 1 Corinthians around AD 55, and therefore he would not have known about the seven trumpets of John described in Revelation, because it was written around AD 90. And if John's seventh trumpet were meant to refer us back to Paul's last trumpet, John probably would have used the term *last trumpet* to make this connection. And he would likely have mentioned the resurrection or rapture.

These two trumpets are distinct symbols used to refer to separate events in God's future plan.

The Time of the Rapture

One of the crucial issues in the interpretation of the rapture is when it will occur. Because the rapture is called a "coming," the tendency has been on the part of many interpreters to equate it with the second coming of Christ, perpetuating the same error that people followed in confusing the first and second comings of Christ in the Old Testament. The Second Coming is clearly preceded by many important events, covering a period of some years (as described in Revelation 6–18 and other passages). By contrast every reference to the rapture in the New Testament pictures it as something that can be expected momentarily with no preceding events revealed.

The idea of an imminent coming of Christ for the church is called the Pretribulation rapture. Those who equate the rapture with the Second Coming are called Posttribulationists. Obviously, from a practical standpoint the question of whether Christ could come today or whether He will not come for many years is a critical item in prophecy and should be determined by careful examination of the Scriptures.

While no one in the Old Testament seems to have understood the difference between the first and second comings of Christ, thousands of interpreters of the New Testament have found the rapture a totally different event than the second coming of Christ. The purpose of the rapture is to take the saints out of the earth to be in heaven while the great end-time events take place on earth. The Second Coming is a totally different event when Christ brings all the saints and angels from heaven to the earthly scene to share in His thousand-year reign on earth.

For instance, the Posttribulational view that the rapture occurs at the time of the Second Coming is built upon the idea that our present troubles are the Great Tribulation. Scriptures are very specific that the Great Tribulation is a three-and-a-half-year period just before the Second Coming, and that it is totally different from our present tribulations. Christ expressed this when He said, "For then there will be great distress, unequaled from the beginning of the world until now—and never to be equaled again" (Matthew 24:21 NIV). He emphasized the unique nature of this period of time by adding, "If those days had not been cut short, no one would survive, but for the sake of the elect those days will be shortened" (24:22 NIV).

The possibility of Christians going through the Great Tribulation is clearly denied by Scripture. The rapture is described in 1 Thessalonians 4:18 as a comfort or inspiring hope, a truth that would be at least partially destroyed if Christians would first have to endure a time of great trouble on earth. It would seem to be obligatory for Paul to have warned the Thessalonians about this. Instead, he told them, "Now, brothers, about times and dates we do not need to write to you, for you know very well that the day of the Lord will come like a thief in the night" (1 Thessalonians 5:1–2 NIV). He compares the hope of the world as being in the darkness of night as opposed to Christians who have the light of day. He states explicitly in 1 Thessalonians 5:9 that the church will not be subject to the wrath of that period, "For God did not appoint us to suffer wrath but to receive salvation through our Lord Jesus Christ" (NIV).

Three Major Rapture Views

Pretribulation Rapture. This view of the timing of the rapture described in 1 Thessalonians 4:17 teaches that before the future seven-year Tribulation, true believers from the church age will be "caught up" from the earth to heaven and therefore be saved from God's wrath during the Tribulation.

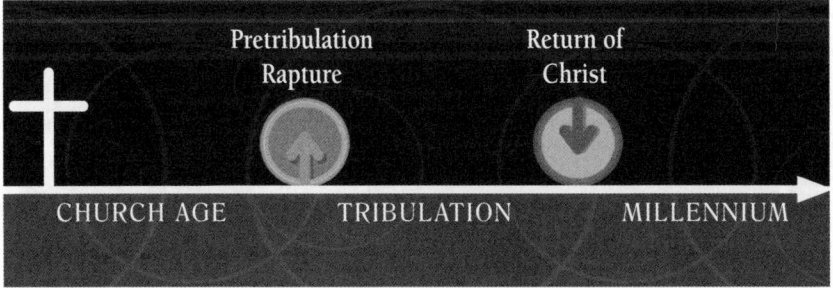

Midtribulation Rapture. This view of the timing of the rapture described in 1 Thessalonians 4:17 teaches that in the middle of the future seven-year Tribulation, true believers will be "caught up" from the earth to heaven, saved from the direct wrath of God that comes during the Great Tribulation.

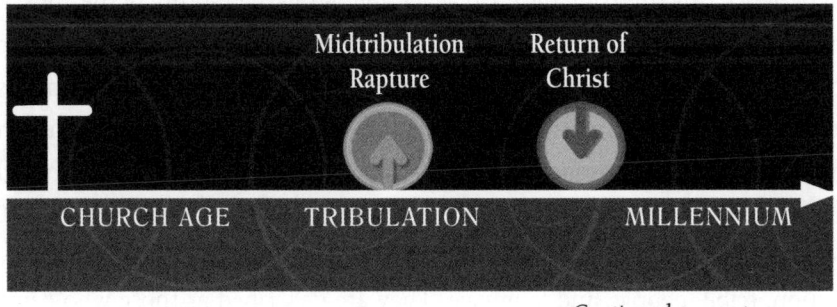

Continued on next page

Continued from previous page

Posttribulation Rapture. This view of the timing of the rapture described in 1 Thessalonians 4:17 teaches that after the future seven-year Tribulation, true believers who survived the persecution and martyrdom of the Great Tribulation will be "caught up" from the earth to heaven, to immediately return to earth to reign with Christ during the Millennium.

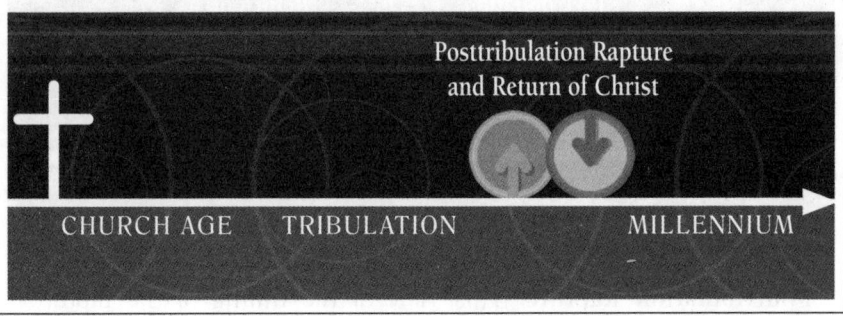

The book of Revelation speaks repeatedly about the Great Tribulation being a time of wrath, but 1 Thessalonians 5:9 denies that the church will experience this time of wrath. However, following the rapture of the church many will come to faith in Christ. These future believers will experience persecution during the Great Tribulation. The book of Revelation makes plain that the world ruler, the Antichrist—who will dominate the earth for three and a half years before the Second Coming—will seek to kill everyone who does not acknowledge him as God (Revelation 13:7, 10, 15). Revelation 7:9–17 pictures a multitude of martyrs in heaven from every nation, tribe, people, and language. They are described as those who came out of the Great Tribulation, apparently martyrs to the faith. These are people who are saved after the rapture and who seal their testimony with their own blood in the Great Tribulation.

Another confirmation that the church will not go through the Tribulation is that the day of the Lord begins at the time of the rapture. The expression "the day of the LORD" is a familiar Old Testament term which refers to any period of time where God deals in direct judgment with Israel because of their waywardness (Joel 1:1–2:17; 3:14–16). Currently the church is in a period of grace in which, in most cases, God is not dealing out direct judgments. Once the rapture of the church occurs, this period ends. Beginning at the rapture and continuing through the tribulation time and the millennial kingdom, Christ "will rule . . . with an iron scepter" (Revelation 19:15 NIV), will put down rebellion, and will judge sin in a drastic and catastrophic way.

The period of the end times extends for approximately seven years from the time of the rapture to the time of the Second Coming. Combining all the Scriptures that bear on the case, Revelation implies that the Roman Empire has to be revived in the end times. According to Daniel 7:7, ten nations band together in what may amount to a United States of Europe or a modern revival of the ancient Roman Empire. This apparently begins as a friendly alliance, but once it is formed a dictator arises (7:8) who first conquers three of the ten countries and then all the rest. Finally, he is regarded as the dominant leader throughout Europe and the Middle East.

During this rise to power he enters into the covenant of Daniel 9:27, which describes a seven-year period leading up to the second coming of Christ. It begins as a peace treaty between Israel and her neighbors, enforced by this new ruler, who is usually identified as the Antichrist. For the first half of the seven years he protects Israel. This peace is shattered when Israel is attacked by an alliance of nations led by a ruler from the north (Ezekiel 38–39). God—not the Antichrist—intervenes and rescues Israel by destroying the invaders.

Will the Real Antichrist Please Stand Up?

Throughout history people have tried to identify the man behind the mark: tagging an individual as the Beast or False Prophet of Revelation 13. One commentator aptly notes, "The number of the beast down through the centuries has been linked with literally hundreds of different possibilities."[1] In Latin, Greek, and Hebrew, letters stand for numbers, so anyone with a calculator and some creativity can paste the "666" label on a number of prominent personalities. The following men have been seriously proposed as being the villain of the end times:

- Titus Flavius Vespasian
- Nero Caesar
- Mohammed
- Constantine
- The popes
- Martin Luther
- Napoleon Bonaparte

- Abraham Lincoln

- Adolf Hitler

- Benito Mussolini

- John F. Kennedy

- Ronald Reagan

- Mikhail Gorbachev

- Saddam Hussein

- Osama bin Laden

As it turns out, none of these men completely fulfilled the job description of Revelation 13. The truth is, we cannot know who the Antichrist will be until he is already in—and out of—control (2 Thessalonians 2:6–8).

At the middle of that last seven years, the Scriptures indicate that the Antichrist will break his covenant with Israel and become their persecutor. He will attempt to kill all Jews and Gentile believers who have chosen to be identified with God rather than to worship him. This begins the period that the Bible specifically calls the Great Tribulation. According to Matthew 24:15, Christ said it would begin with the desecration of a Jewish temple which is yet to be built but which will be in operation at that time. The Antichrist will change the temple into a shrine devoted to the worship of himself. Because he attempts to kill off all who will not worship him as God, God pours out the terrible judgments of Revelation 6–18 which will have the effect of decimating the world's population and destroying its civilization.

Even a casual reading of these chapters reveals how terrible the catastrophes will be. For instance, the fourth seal, which represents an early phase of this judgment, speaks of one-fourth of the earth being destroyed (Revelation 6:7–8). The seal judgments in chapters 6:1–8:1 are followed by a series of punishments heralded by the sounding of seven trumpets. The sixth trumpet adds another terrible fact that one-third of the remaining population of the earth will be killed (9:15). These seven trumpets in turn are followed by the final bowls of God's wrath (16:1–21), each of which is still another terrible judgment on the whole earth.

The seventh and final bowl of wrath is described as an earthquake that is greater than any in history. It will split "the great city," probably Jerusalem, into three parts, and "the cities of the nations collapsed" (Revelation 16:19 NIV). In other words, the nations of the Gentile world are destroyed by this giant earthquake. It is described further as a time in which islands and mountains disappear and the whole earth is in literal convulsions. On top of all this, a supernatural storm pelts the earth with one-hundred-pound hailstones. It would be hard for a fictional story to describe a scene more awful or more destructive of human life and property.

Seals, Trumpets, and Bowls

Three symbols represent three different series of future judgments in the book of Revelation: seven seals, seven trumpets, and seven bowls. Each series describes unique events of the coming Tribulation, and the effects of the judgments overlap so that they intensify toward the end and culminate at the return of Christ.

SEALS
Revelation 6:1–17; 8:1–2

TRUMPETS
Revelation 8:2–9:21; 11:15–19

BOWLS
Revelation 16:1–21

It is only after all this that Jesus Christ will come back in power and glory. As He Himself stated it in Matthew 24:22, one of the purposes of His second coming is to stop the carnage of these terrible judgments which, if allowed to continue, would have destroyed every human person on the earth. It should be obvious that there has never been anything corresponding to this in the history of the world. Once the rapture occurs all creation will plunge into this period of worldwide catastrophe.

The Prophetic Program of God for Israel

A massive program for Israel unfolds as early as Genesis 12, when God promises Abraham that he will be the father of a great nation and a blessing to all peoples on earth. Then in Genesis 12:7, an important prophecy is given: "The LORD appeared to Abram and said, 'To your offspring I will give this land'" (NIV). This is a watershed for prophecy because literalists see this as a promise that God will ultimately give the land to Israel, something that will be fulfilled in the future millennial kingdom after the Second Coming. Those who deny this have to spiritualize this passage and say that the land being promised is not literal. Yet they offer no proof for this assertion. Actually, the word *land* throughout the Old Testament always refers to real estate, and in this instance, to the land of Israel.

God told Abraham that his descendants would leave the land and go to a foreign country. "Know for certain that your descendants will be strangers in a country not their own, and they will be enslaved and mistreated four hundred years. But I will punish the nation they serve as slaves, and afterward they will come out with great possessions" (Genesis 15:13–14 NIV). The first part of this prophecy was fulfilled in the time of Joseph when his family entered Egypt.

Later, as predicted, the nation of Israel left Egypt to return to the Promised Land. Though they wandered in the wilderness for forty years because of unbelief, they conquered at least a part of the land promised to them by God. Before he died, Moses predicted that God would bless Israel as long as they kept the Law. However, if they disobeyed God's commandments, He would drive them from their land (Deuteronomy 28). Sadly, this was fulfilled in the two dispossessions of Israel. The Assyrian armies conquered the ten tribes that became the northern kingdom of Israel and carried them off into captivity in 722 BC. Babylon conquered Jerusalem and the southern kingdom of Judah and forced the remainder of the Jews into exile in Babylon. The Babylonians destroyed the city of Jerusalem, forced Judah's kings off David's throne, and destroyed Solomon's beautiful temple.

In the midst of these catastrophic judgments, however, Jeremiah the prophet gave a ray of hope. "When seventy years are completed for Babylon, I will come to you and fulfill my gracious promise to bring you back to this place" (Jeremiah 29:10 NIV). God had predicted the children of Israel would be carried off to Babylon, and He also predicted they would return.

Ten Biblical Prophecies Yet to Be Fulfilled	
The rapture of the church	John 14:1–3; 1 Corinthians 15:51–52; 1 Thessalonians 4:16–18; Revelation 3:10
The judgment seat of Christ for believers in heaven	1 Corinthians 3:12–15; 2 Corinthians 5:10
The Tribulation	2 Thessalonians 2:3–4; Revelation 6:1–11; 7:9–17; 17:12–13
The rise of the Antichrist and False Prophet	Daniel 7:20, 24; Revelation 13
The world's armies gathering at Armageddon	Joel 3:9–11; Revelation 16:16; 19:17–19
The second coming of Christ	Matthew 24:27–31; Revelation 19:11–16, 19–21
The millennial kingdom	Revelation 20
The great white throne judgment	Revelation 20:11–15
The creation of new heaven and new earth	Revelation 21
The New Jerusalem	Revelation 21:10–27

Many years later Daniel, who had been carried off to Babylon from Jerusalem, read the prophecy of Jeremiah and understood that the desolation of Jerusalem would last seventy years (Daniel 9:2). Knowing the seventy years were almost completed, he immediately started to pray. In one of the beautiful prayers of the Bible, Daniel asked God to answer and fulfill these promises. Not long afterward, the Lord allowed fifty thousand Jews in

Babylon to go back to their Promised Land. In spite of opposition from their enemies, they rebuilt the temple. Yet it was not until ninety years later that Nehemiah encouraged the people to rebuild the wall and eventually the city. All of this was in fulfillment of God's prophecy concerning Israel.

The prophet Jeremiah also predicted that the Jews would come back to their land for a final regathering. He revealed in Jeremiah 30:5–7 that they would go through the Great Tribulation, but he declared, they will be "saved out of it" (NIV). He then announced that Israel would be restored to their land, that David their king would be raised up (compare Ezekiel 34:22–23; 37:24–25), and they would be brought back from the distant places of the earth to occupy their land (Jeremiah 30:8–11). But from AD 70 when the Roman army conquered Jerusalem, destroyed the temple, and scattered the people of Israel all over the earth, until the midpoint of this century, Israel was shut out of their Promised Land. How could God fulfill these Old Testament promises?

In order for God to fulfill the promises of Jeremiah 30—or the covenant of Daniel 9:27 between the future Antichrist and Israel—it was necessary for Israel to go back to their land and organize as a political state. This was fulfilled in 1948. However, while the Israelites who have gone back qualify to fulfill the covenant of Daniel 9, they do not qualify to fulfill the promises of Jeremiah 30 to take possession of the land because they are not believers in Jesus or followers of God.

Here the prophecies of Ezekiel are applicable and describe that God is going to restore Israel, purge out the unbelievers, and allow the righteous to be brought back and installed in their ancient land (Ezekiel 20:33–38). Accordingly, those who are in Israel who are not believers at the second coming of Christ will not be allowed to enter the land. Only godly Israel will inherit the land. The Promised Land will be divided up into twelve parcels, one for each of the twelve tribes (Ezekiel 47:13–48:29). Therefore, God's promise to Abraham that Israel will possess the land as long as the earth lasts will have this graphic and detailed fulfillment in Israel's prophetic program.

A Future for Israel

Many Christians today believe that God's plan for ethnic Israel has come to an end; that the promises of a glorious nation and blessing in the land have been abolished—or perhaps fulfilled in a spiritual sense in the church. Some theologians even propose that Israel has been replaced by the church—utterly rejected, divorced, and without a future in God's plan.

However, the New Testament tells us that God's plan is not to reinterpret the promises for ethnic Israel, but to bring about the fulfillment of those promises through Jesus Christ. Although most of ethnic Israel has been in a state of unbelief since the time of Jesus, God will one day bring a remnant to faith in Christ and restore them in the land promised to their forefathers (Genesis 13:15). Jesus Himself promised the apostles, "In the regeneration when the Son of Man will sit on His glorious throne, you also shall sit upon twelve thrones, judging the twelve tribes of Israel" (Matthew 19:28). Before Christ's ascension, the disciples eagerly inquired about the timing of that earthly kingdom when they asked, "Lord, is it at this time You are restoring the kingdom to Israel?" (Acts 1:6). Jesus did not reject their literal interpretation, but instead He told them that they would not know the timing of the restoration (Acts 1:7–8).

Years later, Paul addressed the problem of the present unbelief of most Jews by declaring that this rebellion would one day be reversed: "A partial hardening has happened to Israel until the fullness of the Gentiles has come in; and so all Israel will be saved" (Romans 11:25–26). In other words, when God has accomplished His purposes through the church, He will again turn His attention to the nation of Israel and bring them to faith in Christ. We can see the beginning of this future for Israel with the sealing of the 144,000 in Revelation 7:1–8.

Why is the restoration of Israel so important? God's very reputation as a promise-keeper is on the line. Paul said, "For the gifts and the calling of God are irrevocable" (Romans 11:29). If we cannot trust God to keep His irrevocable promises to Israel (Jeremiah 31:35–37), then we cannot trust Him to keep His irrevocable promises to us (Romans 8:35–39).

The Prophetic Program for Nations

In the Old Testament, God made numerous predictions concerning the Gentile world. Their history is summarized in the development of six world empires: Egypt, Assyria, Babylon, Medo-Persia, Greece, and Rome. The seventh empire will be the millennial kingdom that God will bring from heaven and will include Gentiles and Jews.

This is all revealed in the book of Daniel. When Daniel interpreted Nebuchadnezzar's great image (Daniel 2), he identified four empires, beginning with Babylon. Later in life Daniel had a series of visions recorded in Daniel 7:1–11:45. Here the four empires are described as four beasts crawling out of the sea. The first beast represented Babylon (7:1–4), the second Medo-Persia (7:5), the third Greece (7:6; 8:21), and the fourth, though not named like the preceding empires, Rome, which was the greatest of the four (7:7–8).

These prophecies have all been fulfilled except the latter stage of the empire of Rome, which seems to coincide with the world empire of the Antichrist in the end times. All these prophecies require careful study to determine what has been fulfilled and what will yet be fulfilled in the future. This whole period is referred to as the times of the Gentiles beginning about 600 BC and ending at the second coming of Christ. At that point, the times of the Gentiles cease and Christ takes over with His millennial kingdom.

Prophecies of the Church in Heaven

Beginning with the rapture, the church is pictured in heaven as the object of God's special grace. Scriptures describe this as a period of wonderful salvation but also as a time of giving an account of life on earth. The church appears before Jesus Christ as its judge, and individual Christians will have their lives evaluated from the standpoint of God's eternal values. Second Corinthians 5:10 declares, "For we must all appear before the judgment seat of Christ, that each one may receive what is due him for the things done while in the body, whether good or bad" (NIV).

This truth is described by three illustrations. In 1 Corinthians 3:10–15, a Christian's life is likened to a building composed of gold, silver, and costly stones or wood, hay, and straw. Only the gold, silver, and costly stones survive the test of fire at this judgment. What escapes the fire will be subject to reward. At this judgment everyone present is a Christian. Their sins have been purged away, they are not condemned, and the judgment has to do only with an evaluation of what in their lives was worthwhile from an eternal standpoint.

First Corinthians 9:24–27 provides a second illustration in which the Christian life is compared to running a race, a common event in Corinth. The Christian, however, is not competing with any other runner but only against the possibilities of what he could be by the grace of God. Accordingly, every Christian can run and win the race. But like a runner, he has to run when God tells him to, and he must avoid distractions that could hinder or even disqualify him. In the end, he will get a crown that will last forever, not one of decaying leaves as was awarded victors in Corinth.

A third illustration is provided in Romans 14:10–12. Here our Christian life is viewed as a trust from God, and like any trust, the trustee is responsible to account for what is given to him even though it does not belong to him. Accordingly, the challenge is to take all that God has provided for us and make it the basis for our faithful life for Him. In connection with this,

He points out how we are not to judge each other as we are not appointed to evaluate the life of another person. We are warned to bow the knee before God and recognize His sovereignty. The matter is summed up in verse 12, "So then, each of us will give an account of himself to God" (NIV). The issue at this judgment will be, "What have you done with what I have given you?"

The rewards are not mentioned in detail in Scripture, but they may be in the form of privileged service in heaven or in the future millennial kingdom as Christians are assigned duties to serve God.

Events That Follow the Second Coming

Clearly, the Second Coming is the beginning of the grand climax of God's purpose for the world. Immediately following the Second Coming is His thousand-year kingdom on earth, to which both the Old and New Testaments ascribe a period of unequalled peace and joy and fulfillment as the world worships the Savior who has returned to the earth. Prophecies for Israel, as well as for the nations, will be fulfilled during this time.

After the thousand-year kingdom in which Satan is bound and rendered inactive, he is loosed again. There will be a worldwide rebellion (Revelation 20:7–9) judged by God with fire from heaven. Immediately after this, Satan is cast into the lake of fire where the Beast and the False Prophet, the leaders of the Great Tribulation, have been in torment for a thousand years. The Scriptures declare, "They will be tormented day and night for ever and ever" (20:10 NIV).

Is Eternal Punishment Biblical?

The concept of never-ending, conscious punishment for unbelievers is unpopular among some Christians. They would prefer to believe that all people are forgiven and will go to heaven one day (universalism) or that the unsaved will simply be destroyed rather than continuing to exist forever (annihilationism). Others see the lake of fire as figurative or metaphorical rather than literal.[2]

Admittedly, the doctrine of never-ending, conscious punishment of the lost is a difficult one to accept mentally and emotionally. However, the Bible is clear that those who choose not to have their sins forgiven through faith in Christ will suffer for eternity in the place prepared for the devil and his angels (Matthew 25:41). Also, we are told the clear fate of those who will worship the Beast during the Tribulation: "And the smoke of their torment goes up forever and ever; they have no rest day and night" (Revelation 14:11).

As difficult and troubling as the doctrine of eternal punishment may be, we must not try to make the Bible say what we want it to say.

The climax of human history will be the judgment of the great white throne (Revelation 20:11–15), in which all the wicked will be raised from the dead. Because they are not recorded in the Book of Life, they will be cast into the lake of fire, an eternal place of punishment for the lost.

Revelation 21–22 describes the new heaven and the new earth created at that time and the New Jerusalem which will rest on the new earth and will be the dwelling place for saints of all ages.

Though history records much rebellion against God and the necessity of God's judgment in time, in the last judgment every wicked deed will be judged, every righteous act will be rewarded, and eternity will be a blessed experience of being in the presence of God for the church and saints of all ages.

The Importance of Prophecy

Obviously, the importance of prophecy is to direct our attention to what is of eternal value in our lives. While salvation is entirely by grace and not by works, rewards are given out only on the basis of what we have done for God, even though we are dependent upon the grace of God for what we do. Accordingly, the Christian life should be constantly looked at as an introduction to our future—a future which goes on forever and is shaped by the importance of what we do in this life for God. The fact that the rapture is imminent and could occur any day puts an urgency behind all that we accomplish for God. What is not accomplished before the rapture will not be accomplished at all.

Prophecy helps believers get ready for future events because after they occur it is too late. In addition to the challenge, however, it is a wonderful hope that we have of being in the glory of God forever with our loved ones in Christ where there will be no sorrow, no sin, and no problems such as we have here.

What Happens to a Person After Death?

"And inasmuch as it is appointed for men to die once and after this comes judgment." (Hebrews 9:27)

	At Death	Bodily Resurrection	Judgment	Eternal Destination
Christian	Christ's Presence The Grave	Resurrection at the Rapture	Judgment Seat of Christ in Heaven	Heaven
Old Testament Believer	Paradise/ Abraham's Bosom The Grave	Resurrection at Christ's Second Coming	Judgment on Earth	Heaven
Tribulation Believer	Christ's Presence The Grave	Resurrection at Christ's Second Coming	Judgment on Earth	Heaven
Unbeliever	Sheol/Hades Torment The Grave	Resurrection at the End of the Millennium	Judgment at the Great White Throne	Hell/ Gehenna/ Lake of Fire

Practical Advice for Perilous Times
by Charles R. Swindoll

Before I was a student at Dallas Theological Seminary, my dad felt that I should learn a trade. So I worked as a machinist's apprentice for four and a half years, serving a trade in which I would later become a journeyman machinist while working my way through school.

During that period of time I got to know a number of interesting people and developed an appreciation for those who earn a living with their hands. That whole blue-collar world is familiar to me, and to this day I recall some wonderful folks I got to know in the shop. One of them was a guy we'll call Tex. This was in Houston, and Tex and I worked second shift along with about three hundred other fellows in a large machine shop. Tex was one of those characters you think of when you think of a machinist. He wore overalls that he changed the oil in about once a month. He had a bandana that hung out of his hip pocket. Every day he wore the same gray-and-white, greasy cap pulled down almost to his ears. I think he changed the oil in the cap about every two years. Same cap, same overalls, same bandana, and in the other hip pocket he had a big pouch of chewing tobacco.

He and I worked on the turret lathes. I worked just behind Tex and would watch him through those hot Houston evenings. He was as predictable as he could be. About thirty minutes after supper, he would reach into his pouch of chewing tobacco. All through the evening, he'd chew that tobacco and he'd spit.

Tex was one of these guys who have unique little phrases about life. People who work in shops like that often sort of boil life down into simple statements. You need to understand, if you've never worked in a shop, that your life is controlled by a whistle. A whistle tells you when work starts. A whistle tells you when it's time for lunch, or for dinner, and a whistle tells you when it's time to go home. It's called "quittin' time." Tex never wore a watch, but he had this inner sensor that let him know the time without even checking. He always knew what time it was, and he would say to me on occasion, "Well, it's 'bout time for supper, Sonny." He always called me Sonny. Sure enough, within a minute or two that whistle would blow. And I always noticed that Tex was ready to go home before anybody else. In fact I said to him one night, "Well, you about ready for quittin' time?" He said, "Sonny, let me tell you somethin'. I stays ready to keeps from gettin' ready. I stays ready for quittin' time." Years passed before I thought about that phrase again. One day while I was in a class at Dallas Theological Seminary studying the events of the future, I recall one of the profs saying he supposed we could call these future things, "when it's quittin' time on earth." And I suddenly remembered Tex's words. "I stays ready to keeps from gettin' ready."

Stay Ready to Keep from Getting Ready

I realize there are all kinds of responses to future things, prophecy, and prophetic events. Some of you probably think it's somewhere between a joke and a leap into a dark room. You're not convinced of any of this, and you're probably reading this out of idle curiosity, wondering what all this prophetic interest is all about. Maybe you were attracted by the subtitle, *Living in the Last Days*. You might, in the back of your mind, be thinking, "I'm not convinced." In fact when you hear words like, "The Lord Himself will descend from heaven with a shout, with the voice of the archangel and with the trumpet of God, and the dead in Christ will rise first" (1 Thessalonians 4:16), you might think, "Wait a minute. You've already lost me. A voice, a shout, a trumpet?" At Dallas Theological Seminary our chaplain, Bill Bryan, plays the trumpet. I often have a lot of fun with Bill as he says the only instrument that's going to be used in heaven is the trumpet. So I found a cute little piece the other day that some wag wrote: "Due to the shortage of trained trumpeters, the end of the world will be postponed three months!"

While some folks choose to laugh about the end times, other people aren't laughing. We recently received a letter from a man who's not laughing, or didn't for a long time, even though I'm sure he passed off things about the future as sort of a joke or something to laugh about. He wrote:

> By the time I had reached my mid-twenties, I was ready to die. I was drinking heavily and participating in all the immoral acts that usually accompany a drunken, selfish, godless lifestyle. Ironically, I had it all. Had a great job, drove a new car, I had, I had, I had, but I truly had nothing. I can't count the number of times during that era that I placed the barrel of a cocked and fully loaded .357 in my mouth or against my head and thought how simple it would be to end it all. That's how it was and that is how it seemed it would always be to me.

Some of you live in a world like that, and when you think about the future you think, "It's kind of a pie-in-the-sky by-and-by that'll meet the needs for some folks, but not me." And then there are those who sort of yawn and think, "I'll kind of lean back and listen because I'm somewhat interested in these kinds of things, but it's really a matter of curiosity for me. I'm not all that concerned about now, and, far as I know, when we die, we'll die like dogs and there won't be any tomorrow."

No one put it better than Billy Graham in his great book *World Aflame*, as he described the complacency of our times:

> In a declining culture, one of its characteristics is that the ordinary people are unaware of what is happening. Only those who know and can read the signs of decadence are posing the questions that as yet have no answers. Mr. Average Man is comfortable in his complacency and as unconcerned as a silverfish ensconced in a carton of discarded magazines on world affairs. He is not asking any questions, because his social benefits from the government give him a false security. This is his trouble and his tragedy. Modern man has become a spectator of world events, observing on his television screen without becoming involved. He watches the ominous events of our times pass before his eyes, while he sips his beer in a comfortable chair. He does not seem to realize what is happening to him. He does not understand that his world is on fire and that he is about to be burned with it.[3]

And then there are those like Tex who can say, "I don't have to get ready. I stay ready." For those of you in that category, the coming of the Lord Jesus represents a sure promise yet to be fulfilled, the anticipated hope that you live your life for—that final dramatic scene when God breaks through the sky and sends His Son, as Dr. Walvoord discussed in the last section. "Then we who are alive and remain shall be caught up together with them in the clouds to meet the Lord in the air. And thus we shall always be with the Lord" (1 Thessalonians 4:17 NKJV).

The Two Comings of Christ: A Study in Contrasts	
At His First Coming . . .	*At His Second Coming . . .*
He came in meekness as a servant (Matthew 20:28).	He will come in power as judge (Matthew 24:30–31; 25:31–46; John 5:26–29).
He came in humility and gentleness (Matthew 11:29; John 5:41).	He will come in majesty and splendor (1 Thessalonians 4:16; Revelation 1:7).
He came to seek and save the lost (Matthew 18:11; Luke 19:10; John 3:17).	He will come to judge and reign (Acts 10:40–42; 2 Corinthians 5:10; Revelation 11:15).
He came to suffer for sinners (Matthew 16:21; 17:12; Mark 9:12).	He will come to rescue the righteous (1 Corinthians 15:51–52; 1 Thessalonians 4:15–17).
He came to sow the seed (Matthew 13:3–9; Luke 8:11).	He will come to reap the harvest (Matthew 13:37–42).

Living in Perilous Times

But that's then, and this is now. What about today? What about now? A. W. Tozer put it in an interesting way. "We think of ourselves as inhabiting a parenthetic interval between the God who was and the God who will be. And we are lonely with an ancient and cosmic loneliness."[4] What about now in the loneliness of today?

As Francis Schaeffer asked, "How should we then live?"[5] I want to build a case for how bad things are today and why we need the promise of a change. Second Timothy 3:1 states, "Realize this, that in the last days difficult times will come." Perilous times. Hard times. The word translated as "difficult" means "hard to bear . . . violent, dangerous."[6] Its only other use in the New Testament is in Matthew 8:28, where Matthew describes two men who had demons and were out of control. They were wild like an untamed animal. Like a storm that's out of control. That's the word used in 2 Timothy for *difficult*: hard borne, storm-tossed. One of my mentors used to refer to this as *savage*. We're living in savage times. It's not that they *will* come, it's that they *have* come.

Think for a moment about the last six, eight, ten months of evening news on the television. Bad times? Hard times? Perilous times? Remember when the playground used to be where kids played? Now it's a battleground. One of my grandchildren told me when we visited his family in California recently, "They've decided that we have to walk through metal detectors now to come to school." He was in sixth grade, going through metal detectors. Remember when we used to play barefoot outside? I remember playing "kick the can" until it was dark. Kicking the can messed my toes up because we were barefooted, but we had a lot of fun. We were playing cops and robbers and nobody even thought anybody would be hurt. No longer. The family is in perilous times.

Stephen Covey, in his book, *The 7 Habits of Highly Effective Families*, breaks our hearts when he writes, "Over the past thirty years the situation for families has changed powerfully and dramatically." As proof, he compiled the following statistics:

- Illegitimate birth rates have increased more than 400 percent.
- The percentage of families headed by a single parent has more than tripled.
- The divorce rate has more than doubled. Many project that about half of all new marriages will end in divorce.
- Teenage suicide has increased almost 300 percent.
- Scholastic Aptitude Test scores among all students have dropped 73 points.
- The number one health problem for American women today is domestic violence. Four million women are beaten each year by their partners.
- One-fourth of all adolescents contract a sexually transmitted disease before they graduate from high school.[7]

Do you know what the problems were in 1940 in the classrooms of the schools? Covey mentions them: Talking out of turn, chewing gum, making noise, running in the halls, cutting in line, dress code infractions, and littering. You know what the problems are in schools today? Covey continues: Drug abuse, alcohol abuse, pregnancy, suicide, rape, robbery, and assault.[8]

How to Live by Faith . . . *While Looking for Christ's Return*[9]

What are we supposed to do before Christ comes? What is our involvement? Our commitment? Three words provide an answer: *occupy, purify,* and *watch.*

Occupy. Even though we believe strongly in Christ's imminent return, and even though we claim to be walking by faith, God has designed specific tasks for us while we wait (2 Thessalonians 3:10–13). We must live responsibly, work diligently, plan wisely, think realistically, and invest carefully.

Purify. Whoever highlights the coming of Christ is also responsible to teach the importance of a pure life. Because He is coming again, there is one thing we want to have in place—personal purity (Titus 2:11–14).

Watch. On several occasions Christ exhorted His disciples to stay on the alert (Mark 13:33–37). God honors those who watch, having a heart that pumps faster when we think of His Son's return (2 Timothy 4:7–8).

Hope Is Needed

Men and women, perilous times have come. We are not getting better and better. Things are not turning out well; they are turning out wrong. We need some hope. We need to know there's a change on the horizon. We also need to know that the Bible addresses how we live in times like these. Generally speaking, words of hope appear all the way through the Gospels. For example, go to Matthew 24. Let me show you some general statements made by our Savior, the Lord Jesus Christ.

If you like marking your Bibles, you may find it interesting to mark repeated statements that are commands to us. Matthew 24:42 says, "Therefore be on the alert, for you do not know which day your Lord is coming." Verse 44 states: "For this reason you also must be ready; for the Son of Man is coming at an hour when you do not think He will." Be on the alert. Be ready.

Look at Mark 13:21–22: "And then if anyone says to you, 'Behold, here is the Christ'; or, 'Behold, He is there'; do not believe him; for false Christs and false prophets will arise, and will show signs and wonders, in order to lead astray, if possible, the elect." From Matthew, we are encouraged to be on the alert. Be ready. Now from Mark, "Take heed; behold, I have told you everything in advance" (13:23). Continue on with verse 33: "Take heed, keep on the alert; for you do not know when the appointed time will come." Verse 35: "Therefore, be on the alert—for you do not know when the master of the house is coming." Verse 37: "What I say to you I say to all, 'Be on the alert!'" Again and again and again, be ready, be on the alert, stay ready, keep ready.

Now go to Luke 21:34–36, "Be on guard, so that your hearts will not be weighted down with dissipation and drunkenness and the worries of life, and that day will not come on you suddenly like a trap; for it will come upon all those who dwell on the face of all the earth. But keep on the alert at all times, praying that you may have strength to escape."

Look at John 14. I love this section of Scripture. Jesus ministers to His disciples. They have followed Him, eaten alongside Him, slept beside Him, watched Him do His work, been mentored by Him, and shared their lives with Him. Now they come to the end in this small upper room, and He unveils to them a plan they were not ready to hear. Verse 1: "Do not let your heart be troubled; believe in God, believe also in Me." And then He turns to the future. He tells them not to be troubled about today. Look to the future. "In My Father's house are many dwelling places; if it were not so, I would have told you; for I go to prepare a place for you. If I go and prepare a place for you, I will come again and receive you to Myself, that where I am, there you may be also" (14:2–3).

Kept from the Hour

Paul said that believers are waiting for Christ to come from heaven; He is the One "who rescues us from the wrath to come" (1 Thessalonians 1:10). What is the *means* by which believers are kept from this coming wrath? He could choose to supernaturally protect us from His judgment, as He did for the Israelites during the plagues in Egypt. Or He could completely remove us from the place of His wrath, as He did with Lot before judging Sodom.

God is not limited to just one way of protecting His people, and He has used a variety of methods in the past. However, in 1 Thessalonians Paul *does* indicate the specific way in which God would save the church from the coming tribulation:

> For the Lord Himself will descend from heaven with a shout, with the voice of the archangel and with the trumpet of God, and the dead in Christ will rise first. Then we who are alive and remain will be caught up together with them in the clouds to meet the Lord in the air, and so we shall always be with the Lord. (1 Thessalonians 4:16–17)

This "catching up" of living believers is directly tied to being saved from wrath several verses later, when Paul wrote, "God has not destined us for wrath, but for obtaining salvation through our Lord Jesus Christ, who died for us, so that whether we are awake or asleep, we will live together with Him" (1 Thessalonians 5:9–10). Given this scriptural background regarding rescue from wrath, it seems best to understand Revelation 3:10 as describing the promise of rescue from the time of tribulation by "catching up" true Christians from the earth. God has many options available for protecting His people from wrath, but in this case, He has chosen to do so by keeping them "from the hour of trial" (Revelation 3:10 NIV), not just protecting them through it.

Marching Orders

It's very surprising to many people that no less than three hundred times in the New Testament alone, future events are mentioned. Three hundred times! In fact, we know more from the Scriptures about hell than about heaven. God is not hesitant to reveal the truth of the future as He predicts and commands us to be ready for what is coming. Now in light of that, return to 2 Timothy 3 for some practical advice for perilous times like these.

What are the marching orders for people who live in these perilous, savage, difficult times when the courts are out of control, when the schools are out of control, when neighborhoods are out of control, when it seems as though even your home at times is out of control? Let me give you four statements that come from the Scriptures we're looking at toward the end of chapter 3 and the early part of chapter 4. How do we stay ready until quittin' time?

First, *follow the model of the faithful*. "Now you followed my teaching, conduct, purpose, faith, patience, love, perseverance, persecutions, and sufferings, such as happened to me at Antioch, at Iconium and at Lystra; what persecutions I endured, and out of them all the Lord rescued me! Indeed, all who desire to live godly in Christ Jesus will be persecuted" (2 Timothy 3:10–12).

You see how Paul put it? You, Timothy, have followed my model. What does it mean to follow the model of the faithful? It means we watch their lives. It means we learn from their example. It means we listen to their instruction. We emulate their virtues. We admire their character. We remember what they endured, and in light of that it helps our endurance. There's something wonderful about having mentors and faithful heroes in the annals of history.

Hebrews 11 is full of those names, and toward the end of that chapter the writer says,

> "What more shall I say? For the time would fail me to tell of [and then he names them] Gideon and Barak and Samson and Jephthah, also of David and Samuel and the prophets: who through faith subdued kingdoms, worked righteousness, obtained promises, stopped the mouths of lions, quenched the violence of fire, escaped the edge of the sword, out of weakness were made strong, became valiant in battle, turned to flight the armies of the aliens. . . . And others were tortured . . . sawn in two. . . . They wandered about in sheepskins and goatskins, being destitute, afflicted, tormented — of whom the world was not worthy." (Hebrews 11:32 – 38 NKJV)

Refuse to believe that because our times are hard there are not people worth following and there are not models worth emulating. There's something inspiring about knowing that someone has gone ahead of us, walked the walk, and lived the life. In light of their example, we can do the same.

I thought about that recently when I came across a story about the Iditarod, an eleven-hundred-mile dogsled race over a part of Alaska in the mid-winter months. You may have read about Susan Butcher who won that race four times. We're talking pioneer woman. She pressed on through the bitter cold and howling winds of a blizzard, dark nights, and exhausting days, as her well-trained huskies pulled her sled over those hundreds of miles from the start to the finish of the race. At the end of one race, she was interviewed and was asked, "How in the world did you stay at it?" You know her answer. "I just remembered that others have done it before me, and I could do it too. Because they did it, so can I." It's unbelievable what she endured. Ten to twelve days in the middle of nowhere, maddening monotony, strained beyond belief. How did she do it? She did it like composers who stay at the music until they get it composed. She did it like people who write books and stay at it until they get all the chapters completed. She did it like mothers of the young who stay at it until they get their children reared and out of the house. She is like all the rest of us. She followed the model of those who have gone before her. And so can you. And so must I.

Men and women, when you get weary of these perilous times, call to mind one of your heroes, one of your mentors. Remember those who have faithfully lived before you and made it, and you can too. Follow the model of the faithful.

Second, *stay with the truth of the Bible.*

> But evil men and imposters will proceed from bad to worse, deceiving and being deceived. You, however, [similar to the "Now you" at the beginning of 2 Timothy 3:10] continue in the things you have learned and become convinced of, knowing from whom you have learned them, [and then Paul gets a very tender thought] and that from childhood you have known the sacred writings which are able to give you the wisdom that leads to salvation through faith which is in Christ Jesus. (2 Timothy 3:13–15)

If you stay with the truth of the Bible, you'll never go wrong. It will never discourage you, and it will never lead you astray. My first thought was to write, "Stay with the teaching of your past," and then I remembered not everyone has been as blessed as I have been, and as many of us have been.

My mind goes back to a little home on Quince Street in East Houston where I was raised. My mother, who loved the Lord dearly, used to challenge us as children to memorize verses of Scripture. She would memorize two verses for every one we would memorize, and when I got into junior high school I thought, "I'm going to show her. I'm going to out-memorize her. I'm going to drive her under the table." So I memorized the book of James. She memorized the book of Hebrews. I decided, "I'm not going there."

Maybe that wasn't your background. Maybe that wasn't the way you were trained or brought up. If not, it's regrettable, because there's something about following, about staying with the teachings of the past. But if that doesn't fit you, how about staying with the truths of the Scriptures? Maybe you didn't have the parents you wish you had. Maybe you don't have a background that you can draw on in days like this. Listen, you've got the Scriptures. Look at Timothy's case, chapter 3 verse 15: "From childhood you have known the sacred writings." *From childhood.* How could that be? I'm glad you asked. Look at 2 Timothy 1:5. Paul again remembers Timothy's past, and he says, "I am mindful of the sincere faith within you, which first dwelt in your grandmother Lois and your mother Eunice, and I am sure that it is in you as well." Timothy had great roots. Paul thinks back to Timothy's grandmother, Lois, and his mother, Eunice. Both of them poured themselves into young Timothy as he was growing up. He learned the ways of God from those in his family.

Go back to 2 Timothy 3:15. Please observe the substance of Timothy's training: "The sacred writings which are able to give you the wisdom that leads to salvation through faith which is in Christ Jesus." Take time to dwell on that. *In these perilous days take time for that Bible class, take time for personal study, take the time to dwell in the Word of God.*

If you didn't have a mother or a grandmother like Timothy had, you can still become like those wise women. I remember helping a church celebrate its fiftieth anniversary. It was a wonderful time of nostalgia. And memories flowed over me. I was blessed to have known Ray Stedman personally as one of his early interns along with Luis Palau. Luis came with his wife, Pat, and their twin babies in 1961, the same year I was there. Luis, Gib Martin, and I poured our lives into that church, and the church into ours. It was wonderful to go back and to celebrate fifty years of history, and it occurred to me how valuable are roots like that and people like Ray Stedman in my life.

While I was there, I was in the home of longtime friends, one of whom is a new grandmother named Sue. She couldn't let go of her little grandbaby. She just held her the whole time she was eating. While she was loving on this little grandbaby and enjoying her, she said, "You know what, Chuck? My role now has changed. I realize now that I am to pour my life into these little ones that my children bring into the world." Isn't that a great perspective?

So I speak to you who are grandparents and great-grandparents. There's something wonderful about passing along the truths of God's Word to those little ones who believe you when you're a grandparent. They just believe you. It's so wonderful you don't have to earn their trust. (Why didn't we have them first? Wouldn't that have been easier?) They just sit and blink their eyes and listen and drink it in. Pour it into them. They're like little birds with their mouths open. And what is it we pour into them? Salvation through faith in Christ Jesus. "All Scripture is inspired by God and profitable for teaching, for reproof, for correction, for training in righteousness" (2 Timothy 3:16). Teaching the truth, refuting error, cultivation of manners in life, and the disciplines in right living. That's what we get from the Scriptures.

In a world where everything has turned gray and become a blur, the Scriptures still mark the lines between right and wrong, between good and evil, between blessed and cursed. Teach your children and grandchildren the Scriptures. Stay with the teachings of the Scriptures.

Third, *proclaim the message of Christ.* "I solemnly charge you in the presence of God and of Christ Jesus, who is to judge the living and the dead,"—there's another future statement, judging the living and the dead—"and by His appearing and His kingdom:"—that's another statement regarding the future, all part of future teaching, all part of God's prophetic plan—"preach the word" (2 Timothy 4:1–2). Proclaim, herald the message. As we move into 2 Timothy 4, we get a little more insight on how to handle perilous times like these.

Follow the model of the faithful. Stay with the truth of the Bible. Proclaim the message of Christ. In an era like this there is no other message like it. Preach the Word. Be ready. Be consistent. Be faithful in season and out of season. Reprove, rebuke, and exhort, but don't be caustic about it. Don't think you can drive it down people's throats. Paul says to do that with great patience and for the purpose of instruction. Proclaim the message of Christ. Press it home, make it clear, say it straight, stand strong.

There's a sense of urgency in these words. For you who are not familiar with the motto of Dallas Theological Seminary, we read it in 2 Timothy 4:2, the first three words. Our motto for over eighty years has remained "Preach the Word." Whenever I walk into Chafer Chapel, I usually turn and look at the wall behind me. There stands the seal of the school. It's a hand holding a torch held high. And around the seal, around this symbol of the torch, are the words written from the Greek text, "Preach the Word." It's a reminder to me on a regular basis that our job is to train men and women to proclaim the message of Christ.

Let me give you a little tip. Individually, you go where none of the rest of us ever go. You touch lives that the person sitting behind you, next to you, or even the one married to you will not touch. You're the one, therefore, who must proclaim the message to your sphere of influence. Paul says to do it in season and out of season. I take that literally. Do it when it's convenient; do it when it's not. Do it in the winter, and do it in the summer. Proclaim it when it's appreciated, and proclaim it when it's resented. Do it when others are open, and do it when others are closed. Whether they are young or old, whether it's early or late, whether it's public or private. When you're asked, and when you're not asked. This is not a biblical mandate for rudeness, for Paul says to do it with patience and to do it for the purpose of instructing (2 Timothy 4:2).

And may I add just a thought here? Keep it simple, very simple. People in perilous times are confused. It's easy for us to dump the truck rather than just giving them a little bit to chew on along with our business card and saying, "This is where you can reach me if you have any more questions about these things we've been talking about." Keep it simple.

One of the many stories that has survived the Civil War has to do with a letter that took only three lines from the president's pen. And yet it was the simple message that changed the course of history and ended the war. It was written by President Lincoln, a man known for plain and simple speech, dated April 7, 1865, 11:00 a.m. It was addressed to General Grant. It read: "Gen. Sheridan says 'If the thing is pressed, I think that Lee will surrender.' Let the *thing* be pressed." Signed, A. Lincoln.[10] By the ninth day of that same month, two days later, Robert E. Lee surrendered at Appomattox Courthouse. The "thing" was pressed.

In these perilous times when there are all kinds of messages and a cacophony of sounds and an assortment of entertainment, all kinds of things attracting our attention, there is something about the simple declaration of the gospel that cuts through all the gobbledy-gook and feeds the hungry heart. Follow the model of the faithful. Stay with the truth of the Bible. Proclaim the message of Christ.

Finally, *maintain an exemplary life.* "For the time will come when they will not endure sound doctrine; [May I for a moment change the words "will come" to "have come" or "has come"? "For the time (*has come*) when they will not endure sound doctrine."] but wanting to have their ears tickled, they will accumulate for themselves teachers in accordance to their own desires, and will turn away their ears from the truth, and will turn aside to myths. But you, [Sound familiar? See 2 Timothy 3:10, 14.] be sober in all things, endure hardship, do the work of an evangelist, fulfill your ministry" (2 Timothy 4:3–5). All the way through this passage Paul is pushing his finger against Timothy's sternum. "You, Timothy. You listen to me, Timothy, listen to me. This is for you." This can be said to you also. "You, however, maintain an exemplary life." There's your fourth marching order.

People can argue with your philosophy, they can deny your theology, they can bring up all kinds of arguments, all kinds of statements that will get you sidetracked, but there's one thing they can never deny, and that's an exemplary life. There is something about a life lived for the glory of God on a campus that the campus will not and cannot ignore. There's something about an exemplary life lived in the office that the people in the office cannot and will not overlook. Maintain an exemplary life. Even though the time has come when people will not endure sound doctrine, Paul says for you to be sober, endure hardship, do the work of an evangelist, fill to the full your ministry. And by the way, we all are engaged in the ministry.

> **'Til His Kingdom Comes . . .**
>
> 1. Follow the Model of the Faithful
> 2. Stay with the Truth of the Bible
> 3. Proclaim the Message of Christ
> 4. Maintain an Exemplary Life

How Can I Stay Ready?

Now, how can I keep this up? How can I make this happen on a regular basis? When the next year turns, when the next century dawns, when I get older and the Lord has not yet returned, what are the timeless facts that I can count on that will help me maintain this sense of readiness? How can I stay ready to keep from getting ready? In each of the last three verses I want you to see there's a principle worth remembering. Look at 2 Timothy 4:6, "I am already being poured out as a drink offering, and the time of my departure has come."

Principle number one. *Consider your life an offering to God rather than a monument to humanity.* The apostle says in the dungeon, "I am already being poured out as a drink offering;" my head is already on the block. It wasn't long before there was the swish of the blade and Paul's head fell from his shoulders. It wasn't long after this ink had dried that the apostle was taken. His life was an offering to God, not a monument to man.

In 4:7, Paul declares: "I have fought the good fight, I have finished the course, I have kept the faith."

Principle number two. *Remember that finishing well is the final proof that truth works.*

Ours is a time of epidemic falling. Falling from the things of Christ. Falling from the privilege of ministry. Let's commit ourselves to being those who finish well. It's great to meet those who are finishing well; it's wonderful. "I've fought the good fight, I've finished the course, I've kept the faith." That's the final proof that truth works.

Paul confidently states in verse 8: "In the future there is laid up for me the crown of righteousness, which the Lord, the righteous Judge, will award to me on that day; and not only to me, but also to all who have loved His appearing." Another reference to the future.

Principle number three. *Fix your eyes on your heavenly reward instead of earthly allurements.* I'm especially fond of the works of C. S. Lewis, as many of you are. I came across a fine statement that I had not heard before. Lewis said about the second coming of Christ, "The great thing is to be found at one's post as a child of God, living each day as though it were our last, but planning as though our world might last a hundred years." [11]

Do you get that? "Living each day as though it were our last, but planning as though our world might last a hundred years." When we do that, we don't have to get ready. We stay ready.

The Five Crowns for Believers
Crown of Exultation 1 Thessalonians 2:19 *For those who win others to Christ*
Crown of Righteousness 2 Timothy 4:8 *For those who look forward to Christ's appearing*
Crown of Life James 1:12; Revelation 2:10; 3:11 *For those who have endured persecution even unto death*
Crown of Imperishability 1 Corinthians 9:25 *For those who run the race of life well*
Crown of Glory 1 Peter 5:4 *For those who lead the church with humility*

Imagine the fulfillment of these words. "The Lord Himself will descend from heaven with a shout, with the voice of the archangel and with the trumpet of God, and the dead in Christ will rise first. Then we who are alive and remain will be caught up together with them in the clouds to meet the Lord in the air, and so we shall always be with the Lord. Therefore, comfort one another with these words" (1 Thessalonians 4:16–18).

If that were to happen right now, would you be ready? Are you absolutely certain that there has been a time in your life when you have said, "I receive the Lord Jesus Christ as my Savior; I take the gift God has offered; I believe He died for my sins; I believe He rose from the dead, bodily, miraculously, and He lives today for me, bringing all into His family who will receive Him as Savior"? If you've never done that, this is the perfect opportunity for you to prepare for what is indeed to come and may come at any moment.

Resources for Digging Deeper

This short book introduces several key issues regarding the end times that could take a lifetime of study to explore. The following resources will help you dig deeper into these important topics. Most of these books should be available from your church library, public library, bookstore, or online bookseller, though some may be out of print. Although we cannot endorse everything a writer asserts, these are some of the more helpful resources for their particular areas of study.

To help you decide which resources are best for you, they have been labeled as "beginner," "intermediate," "advanced," or "expert."

General Works on the End Times

Benware, Paul N. *Understanding End Times Prophecy: A Comprehensive Approach*. Chicago: Moody, 1995. (intermediate)

Hitchcock, Mark. *101 Answers to the Most Asked Questions about the End Times*. Colorado Springs: Multnomah, 2001. (beginner)

Peterson, Eugene H. *Reversed Thunder: The Revelation of John and the Praying Imagination*. San Francisco: HarperSanFrancisco, 1988. (beginner)

Ryrie, Charles C. *Dispensationalism*. Rev. and expanded ed. Chicago: Moody, 1995. (advanced)

Showers, Renald E. *Maranatha: Our Lord, Come! A Definitive Study of the Rapture of the Church.* Bellmawr, N.J.: The Friends of Israel Gospel Ministry, 1995. (intermediate/advanced)

Showers, Renald E. *There Really Is a Difference! A Comparison of Covenant and Dispensational Theology.* Bellmawr, N.J.: The Friends of Israel Gospel Ministry, 1990. (advanced)

Swindoll, Charles R., John F. Walvoord, and J. Dwight Pentecost. *The Road to Armageddon: A Biblical Understanding of Prophecy and End Time Events.* Nashville: Word, 1999. (beginner/intermediate)

Walvoord, John F. *End Times: Understanding Today's World Events in Biblical Prophecy.* Swindoll Leadership Library, ed. Charles R. Swindoll. Nashville: Word, 1998. (beginner/intermediate)

Willis, Wesley R. and John R. Master, eds. *Issues in Dispensationalism.* Chicago: Moody Press, 1994. (expert)

Zuck, Roy B., ed. *Vital Prophetic Issues: Examining Promises and Problems in Eschatology.* Grand Rapids: Kregel, 1995. (intermediate/advanced)

Commentaries and Reference Works on the Book of Revelation

Ryrie, Charles C. *Revelation.* New ed. Everyman's Bible Commentary. Chicago: Moody, 1996. (intermediate)

Stedman, Ray C., and James D. Denney. *God's Final Word: Understanding Revelation.* Grand Rapids: Discovery House, 1991. (beginner)

Thomas, Robert L. *Revelation 1–7: An Exegetical Commentary*. Chicago: Moody, 1992. (advanced/expert)

Thomas, Robert L. *Revelation 8–22: An Exegetical Commentary*. Chicago: Moody, 1995. (advanced/expert)

Walvoord, John F. *The Revelation of Jesus Christ*. Chicago: Moody, 1966. (advanced)

Differing Views on the End-Times Issues

Archer, Gleason L., Jr., ed. *Three Views on the Rapture: Pre-, Mid-, or Post-Tribulation*. Grand Rapids: Zondervan, 1996. (intermediate/advanced)

Bock, Darrell L., ed. *Three Views on the Millennium and Beyond*. Grand Rapids: Zondervan, 1999. (intermediate/advanced)

Crockett, William, ed. *Four Views on Hell*. Counterpoints. Grand Rapids: Zondervan, 1996. (intermediate/advanced)

Erickson, Millard J. *A Basic Guide to Eschatology: Making Sense of the Millennium*. Rev. ed. Grand Rapids: Baker Book House, 1998. (advanced)

Pate, C. Marvin, ed. *Four Views on the Book of Revelation*. Grand Rapids: Zondervan, 1998. (intermediate/advanced)

Glossary of Terms

144,000: A remnant of the people of Israel, chosen by God during the future **Tribulation** to be witnesses of Christ and to fulfill God's promise of a restored nation of Israel during the **Millennium**. See Revelation 7:1–8 and 14:1–5.

Allegorical Interpretation: The approach to reading Scripture that sees stories of the Bible as symbolic representations or illustrations of deeper moral or spiritual truths. It is a type of **non-literal interpretation**.

Amillennialism: The perspective, held by many theologians since Augustine in the fourth century, that understands the **Millennium** described in Revelation 20:4–6 as occurring presently and spiritually either through Christ's reign at the right hand of God or through the righteousness of the **church**. Thus, those who hold this view deny that Christ will reign over a literal, earthly kingdom after His **second coming**. Amillennialists often use a **non-literal interpretation** of various Scripture passages that refer to an earthly kingdom.

Antichrist: The future end-time dictator who will claim to be God, attempt to destroy Israel, persecute believers in Christ, and establish a godless empire over the earth during the **Great Tribulation**. Also called the Beast from the sea or the "man of lawlessness." See Daniel 9:26–27; 2 Thessalonians 2:3–12; Revelation 13:1–8.

Apocalypse: From the Greek word *apokalupsis*, this refers to a revealing, or unveiling, of something previously hidden. The book of Revelation, or "The Apocalypse of John," is an unveiling of future events (Revelation 1:1).

Armageddon: During this last battle of the **Tribulation**, the armies of the **Antichrist** and other kings gather to make war in the region known as Megiddo in northern Israel. However, they will be instantly destroyed by Christ at His **second coming**. See Revelation 16:13–16; 19:19–21.

Beast from the Earth: See **False Prophet**.

Beast from the Sea: See **Antichrist**.

Bowl Judgments: The final judgments of God's **wrath** are poured out on the earth as described in Revelation 16. Also known as the "bowls of wrath," these judgments immediately follow the **trumpet judgments** and precede the **second coming** of Christ.

Church: The ever-enlarging universal church is made up of all true believers in heaven and on earth over whom Jesus Christ reigns as Lord. Regardless of denomination, all true believers are spiritually baptized by the Holy Spirit into Christ's body and are therefore spiritually united with Him and with one another. See Romans 12:4–5; 1 Corinthians 12:12–14; Ephesians 4:11–16; and 1 Peter 2:9–10.

Church Age: The period of time in which the **church** stands at the center of God's unfolding plan for human history, during which the gospel is preached and disciples are made in Christ-following communities united by the Holy Spirit. The church age extends from the day of Pentecost (Acts 2) and will continue until the **rapture** of the church (1 Thessalonians 4:17).

Dead in Christ: Believers in Christ who have died and whose spirits are currently in heaven, awaiting the resurrection of their physical bodies. See 1 Thessalonians 4:15–16.

Eschatology: From the Greek words *eschatos*, "last," and *logos*, "discourse," eschatology is the study of "last things"—the study of the end times, including prophecies relating to future events in God's plan.

False Prophet: The religious/spiritual deceiver and cohort of the **Antichrist** during the **Great Tribulation**; also called the Beast from the earth. See 2 Thessalonians 2:9–11 and Revelation 13:11–18.

Figurative Language: Language used in normal speech that is intended by the speaker or author to convey literal truth through metaphors, wordplay, symbols, or allegory. Those who practice **literal interpretation** of Scripture acknowledge the use of figurative language as an author-intended means of communicating literal truth.

First Resurrection: See **Resurrection, First**.

Great Tribulation: The last three and a half years of the seven-year **Tribulation** period, characterized by the reign of the **Antichrist**, severe persecution and martyrdom, and the pouring out of God's **bowl judgments**.

Great White Throne: According to Revelation 20:11–15, all the unsaved who have ever lived will be resurrected to stand before God's great white throne to receive their sentencing. There will be no appeal, no debate over guilt or innocence, no final offer of clemency, and no possibility of escape. All who attend this judgment will spend eternity in hell.

Literal Interpretation: In contrast with **allegorical interpretation** and **non-literal interpretation**, this approach to understanding the Bible focuses on the normal, face-value meaning of the words and passages in their historical and cultural context, with an emphasis on the author's original intent and with a sensitivity toward different types of literature such as prose, poetry, history, and prophecy, and the use of **figurative language**.

Messianic Kingdom: See **Millennium**.

Midtribulation Rapture: This view of the timing of the **rapture** described in 1 Thessalonians 4:17 teaches that in the middle of the future seven-year **Tribulation**, true believers will be "caught up" from the earth to heaven, saved from the direct **wrath** of God that comes during the **Great Tribulation**.

Millennial Kingdom: See **Millennium**.

Millennium: From the Latin words *mille*, "thousand," and *annus*, "year," this is the thousand-year reign of Christ with His saints as described in Revelation 20:1–5, during which time Satan is bound. Some interpreters understand the Millennium to be a literal kingdom that will be established in the future (**premillennialism**), while others take it figuratively as referring to a current or ideal spiritual state (**amillennialism** or **postmillennialism**).

New Heaven and New Earth: The sin-damaged earth will be destroyed and re-created. And according to Revelation 21:1–22:5, God will create a new heaven and earth where the redeemed from throughout history will live forever with Him.

Non-literal Interpretation: In contrast with **literal interpretation**, the non-literal method of biblical interpretation seeks a hidden, deeper, or spiritualized meaning of the words of Scripture different from the normal, face-value meaning intended by the original author and understood by the original audience.

Postmillennialism: This view understands the **Second Coming** to occur after the **Millennium**, which is interpreted as the present reign of Christ on the earth through the social and political influence of the gospel. Postmillennialism has often been associated with the "social gospel" of liberal theology—the view that biblical principles are meant to transform society, culture, and governments, not just individuals and the church.

Posttribulation Rapture: This view of the timing of the **rapture** described in 1 Thessalonians 4:17 teaches that after the future seven-year **Tribulation**, true believers who survived the persecution and martyrdom of the **Great Tribulation** will be "caught up" from the earth to heaven, to immediately return to earth to reign with Christ during the **Millennium**.

Premillennialism: This millennial view understands the **Second Coming** to occur before the **Millennium**, which is understood as a literal reign of Christ and all true believers on earth after the **Tribulation**. Premillennialists hold that the **first resurrection** will occur in two stages—all believers will be resurrected before the **Millennium**, joining those believers who survive the **Tribulation**, and will receive their rewards at this time; all unbelievers will be resurrected after the **Millennium** and judged.

Preterism: The view that regards most of the biblical prophecies, including the visions of the book of Revelation, to have already been fulfilled in the first- or early second-century persecutions and wars. Preterists do not anticipate a future **Tribulation**, **Antichrist**, or other end-time events.

Pretribulation Rapture: This view of the timing of the **rapture** described in 1 Thessalonians 4:17 teaches that before the future seven-year **Tribulation**, true believers from the **church age** will be "caught up" from the earth to heaven and therefore be saved from God's **wrath** during the **Tribulation**.

Rapture (of the Church): The *rapture* refers to the "catching up" to heaven of all believers—both the living and the dead—as described in 1 Thessalonians 4:17. Different views on the timing of the rapture in relation to the **Tribulation** include **Pretribulation, Midtribulation,** and **Posttribulation**.

Reign of Christ: See **Millennium**.

Remnant of Israel: See **144,000**.

Resurrection, First: The resurrection of the true believers of all history, which takes place in several stages. It began with the resurrection of Jesus Christ and will include the resurrections of the **church**, the Old Testament saints, and the **Tribulation saints**. See Revelation 20:5–6.

Resurrection, Second: The resurrection of the unsaved of all history, which takes place at the **great white throne**, for the purpose of judgment according to their works. All those who take part in the second resurrection will be thrown into the lake of fire for all eternity (Revelation 20:11–15).

Return of Christ: See **Second Coming**.

Seal Judgments: The first series of God's judgments during the **Tribulation**, as described in Revelation 6, which are immediately followed by the **trumpet judgments** (Revelation 8:1–2).

Second Coming: The coming of Christ in glory—as described in Revelation 19:11–21—to judge the nations, to complete the **first resurrection** of the righteous saints, and to establish the **millennial kingdom**. Those who hold to a **Pretribulation rapture** distinguish between Christ's coming "in the air" to **rapture** the church and His second coming to earth in judgment and to reign as King.

Tribulation: Besides a reference to the general trouble, trials, and persecutions that all Christians endure throughout the **church age** (John 16:33), the term *Tribulation*, when referring to the end times, refers to the final, seven-year period of judgments described in Daniel 9:27; Matthew 24:1–28; and Revelation 11–13. The **Great Tribulation** is often used to refer to the last three and a half years of the Tribulation.

Tribulation Saints: For those who hold to a **Pretribulation rapture**, the Tribulation saints are those who trust Christ for their salvation after the **rapture** of the **church** and during the seven-year **Tribulation** period.

Trumpet Judgments: The second series of God's judgments during the **Tribulation**, immediately after the **seal judgments** and preceding the **bowl judgments**, as described in Revelation 8:1–11:19.

Wrath: God's righteous anger toward the ungodliness and unrighteousness of humanity, based on His holiness and justice (Romans 1:18). Though God will exercise His final wrath against the sinful world through a series of intensifying judgments during the coming **Tribulation**, Christians are promised to be saved from His wrath (1 Thessalonians 1:10; 5:9). The means of this salvation from wrath is the **rapture** of the **church** (1 Thessalonians 4:15–18).

How to Begin a Relationship with God

Many people associate the book of Revelation with visions of fire and brimstone, but sometimes they forget that Revelation is filled with profound promises. To those who "overcome," Christ personally offers eternal life, a guaranteed inheritance, the prospects of reigning as royalty over the earth, and freedom from suffering, sorrow, and death (Revelation 2:7, 11, 17, 26; 3:5, 12, 21). Who are the ones who "overcome"? Are they super-saints who live unblemished lives? Do they work hard enough to earn their own reward? Have they suffered and died for the faith? Do they attend the right church and go through the right rituals? The apostle John makes it clear who these victorious ones really are: "Who is the one who overcomes the world, but he who believes that Jesus is the Son of God?" (1 John 5:5).

To understand how you can begin a relationship with God and join those who "overcome," we need to back up from the end of the story and consider the beginning. The most marvelous book in the world, the Bible, marks the path to God with four vital truths. Let's look at each marker in detail.

Our Spiritual Condition: Totally Depraved

The first truth is rather personal. One look in the mirror of Scripture, and our human condition becomes painfully clear:

There is none righteous, not even one;
There is none who understands,
There is none who seeks for God;
All have turned aside, together they have become useless;
There is none who does good,
There is not even one. (Romans 3:10–12)

We are all sinners through and through—totally depraved. Now, that doesn't mean we've committed every atrocity known to humankind. We're not as *bad* as we can be, just as *bad off* as we can be. Sin colors all our thoughts, motives, words, and actions.

You still don't believe it? Look around. Everything around us bears the smudge marks of our sinful nature. Despite our best efforts to create a perfect world, crime statistics continue to soar, divorce rates keep climbing, and families keep crumbling.

Something has gone terribly wrong in our society and in ourselves—something deadly. Contrary to how the world would repackage it, "me-first" living doesn't equal rugged individuality and freedom; it equals death. As Paul said in his letter to the Romans, "The wages of sin is death" (Romans 6:23)—our spiritual and physical death that comes from God's righteous judgment of our sin, along with all of the emotional and practical effects of this separation that we experience on a daily basis. This brings us to the second marker: God's character.

God's Character: Infinitely Holy

How can a good God judge the world with the wrath described in Revelation? To bring it closer to home, how can God judge each of us for a sinful state we were born into? Our total depravity is only half the answer. The other half is God's infinite holiness.

The fact that we know things are not as they should be points us to a standard of goodness beyond ourselves. Our sense of injustice in life on this side of eternity implies a perfect standard of justice beyond our reality. That standard and source is God Himself. And God's standard of holiness contrasts starkly with our sinful condition.

Scripture says that "God is Light, and in Him there is no darkness at all" (1 John 1:5). God is absolutely holy—which creates a problem for us. If He is so pure, how can we who are so impure relate to Him?

Perhaps we could try being better people, try to tilt the balance in favor of our good deeds, or seek out methods for self-improvement. Throughout history, people have attempted to live up to God's standard by keeping the Ten Commandments or living by their own code of ethics. Unfortunately, no one can come close to satisfying the demands of God's law. Romans 3:20 says, "For no one can ever be made right with God by doing what the law commands. The law simply shows us how sinful we are" (NLT).

Our Need: A Substitute

So here we are, sinners by nature and sinners by choice, trying to pull ourselves up by our own bootstraps to attain a relationship with our holy

Creator. But every time we try, we fall flat on our faces. We can't live a good enough life to make up for our sin, because God's standard isn't "good enough"—it's *perfection*. And we can't make amends for the offense our sin has created without dying for it.

Who can get us out of this mess?

If someone could live perfectly, honoring God's law, and would bear sin's death penalty for us—in our place—then we would be saved from our predicament. But is there such a person? Thankfully, yes!

Meet your substitute—*Jesus Christ*. He is the One who took death's place for you!

> [God] made [Jesus Christ] who knew no sin to be sin on our behalf, so that we might become the righteousness of God in Him. (2 Corinthians 5:21)

God's Provision: A Savior

God rescued us by sending His Son, Jesus, to die for our sins on the cross (1 John 4:9–10). Jesus was fully human and fully divine (John 1:1, 18), a truth that ensures His understanding of our weaknesses, His power to forgive, and His ability to bridge the gap between God and us (Romans 5:6–11). In short, we are "justified as a gift by His grace through the redemption which is in Christ Jesus" (Romans 3:24). Two words in this verse bear further explanation: *justified* and *redemption*.

Justification is God's act of mercy, in which He declares believing sinners righteous, while they are still in their sinning state. Justification doesn't mean that God *makes* us righteous, so that we never sin again, rather that He *declares* us righteous—much like a judge pardons a guilty criminal. Because Jesus took our sin upon Himself and suffered our judgment on the cross, God forgives our debt and proclaims us PARDONED.

Redemption is God's act of paying the ransom price to release us from our bondage to sin. Held hostage by Satan, we were shackled by the iron chains of sin and death. Like a loving parent whose child has been kidnapped, God willingly paid the ransom for you. And what a price He paid! He gave His only Son to bear our sins—past, present, and future. Jesus's death and resurrection broke our chains and set us free to become children of God (Romans 6:16–18, 22; Galatians 4:4–7).

Placing Your Faith in Christ

These four truths describe how God has provided a way to Himself through Jesus Christ. Because the price has been paid in full by God, we must respond to His free gift of eternal life in total faith and confidence in Him to save us. We must step forward into the relationship with God that He has prepared for us—not by doing good works or being a good person, but by coming to Him just as we are and accepting His justification and redemption by faith.

> For by grace you have been saved through faith; and that not of yourselves, it is the gift of God; not as a result of works, so that no one may boast. (Ephesians 2:8–9)

We accept God's gift of salvation simply by placing our faith in Christ alone for the forgiveness of our sins. Would you like to enter a relationship with your Creator by trusting in Christ as your Savior? If so, here's a simple prayer you can use to express your faith:

Dear God,

I know that my sin has put a barrier between You and me. Thank You for sending Your Son, Jesus, to die in my place. I trust in Jesus alone to forgive my sins, and I accept His gift of eternal life. I ask Jesus to be my personal Savior and the Lord of my life. Thank You. In Jesus's name, amen.

If you've prayed this prayer or one like it and you wish to find out more about knowing God and His plan for you in the Bible, contact us at Insight for Living. You can speak to one of our pastors on staff by calling 972-473-5097. Or you can write to us at the address below.

As you ponder your personal destiny in light of the book of Revelation, no other decision can compare with the one that puts you in a right relationship with God through His Son, Jesus Christ, who loved us and gave Himself for us.

Insight for Living
Pastoral Ministries Department
Post Office Box 269000
Plano, Texas 75026-9000

We Are Here for You

If you desire to find out more about knowing God and His plan for you in the Bible, contact us. Insight for Living provides staff pastors and women's counselors who are available for free written correspondence or phone consultation. These seminary-trained and seasoned men and women have years of pastoral experience and are well-qualified guides for your spiritual journey.

Please feel welcome to contact our Pastoral Ministries department by calling the Insight for Living Care Line: 972-473-5097, Monday through Friday, 8:00 a.m.–5:00 p.m. Central time. Or you may write to the following address:

Insight for Living
Pastoral Ministries Department
Post Office Box 269000
Plano, Texas 75026-9000

Endnotes

1. Grant R. Osborne, *Revelation*, Baker Exegetical Commentary on the New Testament, ed. Moisés Silva (Grand Rapids: Baker Academic, 2002), 519.

2. For various views on hell, see William Crockett, ed., *Four Views on Hell*, Counterpoints (Grand Rapids: Zondervan, 1996).

3. Billy Graham, *World Aflame* (Garden City, N.Y.: Doubleday, 1965), 16–17. © Copyright 1965 by Billy Graham. Used by permission. All rights reserved.

4. A. W. Tozer, *The Divine Conquest* (Camp Hill, Pa.: Christian Publications, 1950), 23.

5. Francis A. Schaeffer, *How Should We Then Live? The Rise and Decline of Western Thought and Culture* (Westchester, Ill.: Crossway Books, 1976).

6. Walter Bauer and others, eds., *A Greek-English Lexicon of the New Testament and Other Early Christian Literature*, 2d rev. ed. (Chicago: University of Chicago Press, 1979), 874.

7. Stephen R. Covey, *The 7 Habits of Highly Effective Families: Building a Beautiful Family Culture in a Turbulent World* (New York: Golden Books, 1997), 17. Used by permission of The FranklinCovey Company.

8. Covey, *The 7 Habits of Highly Effective Families*, 17. Used by permission of The FranklinCovey Company.

9. Adapted from Charles R. Swindoll, "How to Live by Faith . . . While Looking for Christ's Return," *Insights*, vol. 8, no. 4 (April 1998), 1–2.

10. Abraham Lincoln to Ulysses S. Grant, April 7, 1865, in *Collected Works of Abraham Lincoln*, ed. Roy P. Bosler (New Brunswick: N.J.: Rutgers University Press, 1953), http://name.umich.edu/lincoln8 (accessed December 29, 2006).

11. Sherwood E. Wirt, "Heaven, Earth and Outer Space: Part Two of an Interview with C. S. Lewis," *Decision* (October 1963), 4.

Ordering Information

If you would like to order additional copies of *'Til His Kingdom Comes: Living in the Last Days* or order other Insight for Living resources, please contact the office that serves you.

United States

Insight for Living
Post Office Box 269000
Plano, Texas 75026-9000
USA
1-800-772-8888 (Monday through Thursday, 7:00 a.m.–9:00 p.m., and Friday, 7:00 a.m.–7:00 p.m.)
www.insight.org

Canada

Insight for Living Canada
Post Office Box 2510
Vancouver, BC V6B 3W7
CANADA
1-800-663-7639
www.insightforliving.ca

Australia and South Pacific

Insight for Living Australia
Post Office Box 1011
Bayswater, VIC 3153
AUSTRALIA
1 300 467 444
www.insight.asn.au

United Kingdom and Europe

Insight for Living United Kingdom
Post Office Box 348
Leatherhead
KT22 2DS
UNITED KINGDOM
0800 915 93 64
www.insightforliving.org.uk

Other International Locations

International constituents may c
the U.S. office through our Web
(www.insight.org), mail querie
calling 972-473-5136.